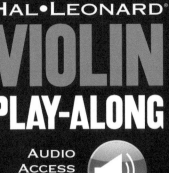

HAL•LEONARD®
VIOLIN
PLAY-ALONG

AUDIO
ACCESS
INCLUDED

Stephane Grappelli

CONTENTS

To access audio visit:
www.halleonard.com/mylibrary

8655-7381-5999-6829

ISBN 978-1-4234-8647-3

HAL•LEONARD®
CORPORATION
7777 W. BLUEMOUND RD. P.O. BOX 13819 MILWAUKEE, WI 53213

Visit Hal Leonard Online at
www.halleonard.com

Cover photo: Jan Perrson/CTS Images

Violin - Jerry Loughney
Guitar - Kirk Tatnall
Bass - Brian Baker
Drumset, piano - Dan Maske

Recorded and Produced by Dan Maske

Django

By John Lewis

It Don't Mean a Thing
(If It Ain't Got That Swing)

Words and Music by Duke Ellington and Irving Mills

Minor Swing

By Django Reinhardt and Stephane Grappelli

Limehouse Blues

from ZIEGFELD FOLLIES

Words by Douglas Furber
Music by Philip Braham

Nuages

By Django Reinhardt and Jacques Larue

Ol' Man River

from SHOW BOAT

Lyrics by Oscar Hammerstein II
Music by Jerome Kern

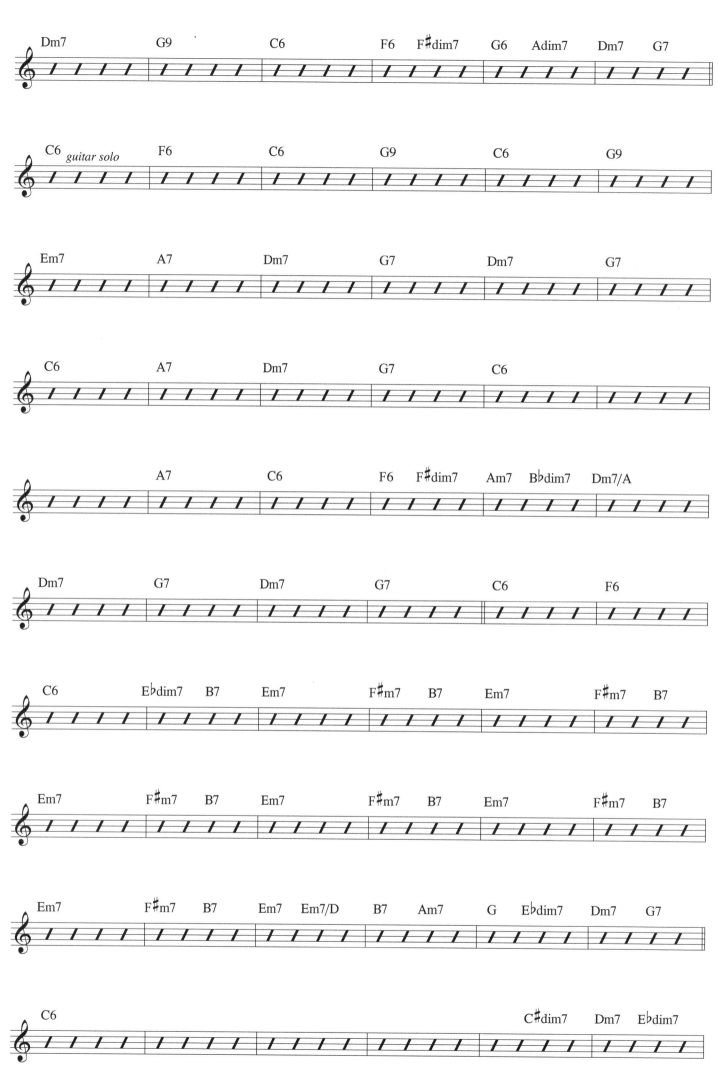

The Way You Look Tonight

Words by Dorothy Fields
Music by Jerome Kern

Stardust

Words by Mitchell Parish
Music by Hoagy Carmichael